Paperback ISBN: 9798218059781

eBook ISBN: 9798218059798

Artwork & design by Bob Bjarke

Type set in 11-point Egenolff-Berner Garamond Regular

 Non-Goals Fan Club, est. 2021
NonGoalsFC.com

Printed in the United States of America

1st Printing

CONTENTS

NON-GOALS

What to look for when you're
looking at soccer.

OAKLAND, California

Ostensibly Books, Publishers

2022.

For Katie, Otto, and Alex.

INTRODUCTION

I remember watching the 1998 World Cup almost exclusively for the commercials. Well really just for one specific commercial. It was a Nike ad, and in it the Brazilian national soccer team scrimmages through a busy airport, annoying security guards, kicking balls through x-ray machines, and dancing their way down moving walkways with a ball at their feet. It's a delightful ninety seconds, and it perfectly captures the joy those 1990s Brazilian teams played with as they pulled one magic trick out of their hats after another, almost always making a World Cup trophy appear at the end.

I didn't grow up a soccer fan. My brothers and I sat through some of those '98 World Cup games, hoping the Nike spot would appear at halftime, trying to pick out the Spanish words we knew as we listened to the Spanish-language commentary on TV (Telemundo carried most of the games in our area), but we didn't know the game and if it hadn't been summer time we probably wouldn't have tuned in. As a kid growing up in rural central California, I was obsessed with American sports: baseball, basketball, and football. It wasn't until the 2006 World Cup, when I shared a big apartment in Chicago with a rotating cast of French students that I really started to understand the game and develop a taste for it. As I spent time watching the tournament with my European friends I was drawn to the skill and endurance of the players, the clear stylistic differences of the national teams, and the musical sounds of the Italian squad's names (say them out loud: "Cannavaro, Zambrotta, Ambrosini, Luca Toni, Cameronesi!"). Fast-forward twenty-five years, thousands of soccer games watched on TV and in person, and soccer is unquestionably the sport I love watching more than any other.

Years later, it's taken me a long time to understand why. There are some clear superficial elements that make the soccer viewing experience great: no commercials during the game, no timeouts to slow things

*Scenes from the 1998 Nike commercial
featuring Brazil's selecao.*

down in crucial moments, and most games are done in a tidy two hours. It also doesn't hurt that I started watching soccer at a great moment in history. There have never been more soccer games on American TV, access to soccer news and analysis online feed a hungry audience, and the Leo Messi and Cristiano Ronaldo era, in which two of the greatest players ever regularly square off against each other on the largest stages, has been in full swing for the last 15 years and is only beginning to wind down.

But as I started watching more soccer I noticed that the game was holding my attention more than others. Even as I found myself reaching for my iPhone while watching NBA games in the 2010s, I didn't have that urge while watching soccer. As I understood more about the game, I realized I was watching the sport in a totally different way than I had any other. I loved seeing goals, and having chosen FC Barcelona as my favorite team there were plenty of those to see, but I realized I often loved the moments that weren't goals just as much as the goals themselves. I observed that a goal was sometimes the anticlimactic end of a spectacular passage of play, and that the most impressive part of the goal might have happened many seconds before the ball crossed the goal line. The most amazing part of a game might have been the way a defender craftily stole the ball and began a counter attack. Or the way a midfielder managed to find a gap in the defense that nobody else saw and passed through it. Or how a striker might make a run through the opponent's defense to make space for their teammates. And how, without ever touching the ball, that striker and their movement created the opportunity for a shot or a goal.

While goals can be terrific and sublime, they're just as often totally forgettable: goals that come in from a corner kick and ricochet around the box before somehow bouncing in; hopeful, long-distance strikes that deflect off defenders' backs, changing course mid-flight and eventually floating past the unlucky keeper. This variety of goal is fairly common, altering the face of a match without really deserving to.

At some point it dawned on me—I fell in love with soccer when I stopped focusing on outcomes like wins and goals. Soccer is a game that ends without a winner about 20% of the time. A game in which nobody wins occurs 1 in every 5 games in the Premier League, often considered the most competitive league in the world. In the Champions League that number is closer to 50%. A World Cup game ends in a draw about 25% of the time. According to American Soccer Analysis, goals happen on about 10% of all shots and shots happen on about 11% of all possessions. If a team earns about 140 possessions a game, on average, that means teams score about 1.23 goals per game. Looking for outcomes while watching soccer is counterproductive because outcomes are elusive. But what you will almost always witness while watching soccer are passages of play that blow your mind, individual moments of brilliance that seem impossible at first glance but really happened, tactical adjustments that unlock the opposing team's defense, the list goes on.

After a while I started thinking of these moments as "non-goals." Borrowing a term from the tech world that usually means something you meaningfully set out not to accomplish, I wanted to draw attention to this counterintuitive approach to watching sports. I hope that readers come away from this book with the idea that soccer is a lot deeper than the score or the final result, and that they're able to find enjoyment in looking for the non-goals of the game—the brilliant, skillful, inspiring moments between scoring that can hold your attention for hours or, in my case, years. If you can rewire your brain to love non-goals, you'll find a new appreciation for a sport with an almost infinite supply of great moments in every match, season, league, and tournament.

As the Brazilian team weaves their way through the crowded airport terminal in that Nike commercial, disrupting boarding groups and impressing awe-stuck children, their star striker, Ronaldo, spots two retractable barricades a few feet apart in the distance—the perfect makeshift goal to strike the ball though at the end of his team's flowing display. Taking aim, he smashes his foot through the ball, and watches as his shot sails toward its target before hitting the right hand post and bouncing back toward him. He grimaces, the once captivated kids cover their eyes in disappointment, the Nike logo appears, and the spot is over. No goal.

INTO SPACE

In 1962 President John F. Kennedy delivered a speech to 40,000 people at the most sacred of all American institutions: a football stadium in Texas. In this speech he set forth his vision for "landing a man on the Moon and returning him safely to the Earth" that would take place before the end of the decade.

But why choose the moon, he asked? Well, "why climb the highest mountain? Why, 35 years ago, fly the Atlantic? Why does Rice play Texas?" (Kudos to JFK for maybe the world's greatest example of playing to the crowd.)

"We choose to go to the Moon in this decade and do the other things, not because they are easy, but because they are hard," he continued, noting that this endeavor "will serve to organize and measure the best of our energies and skills."

Many say landing on the moon was mankind's greatest achievement. While that's likely to be true, I submit the pass into space (or the "through ball" for the less astronomically inclined) as the soccer equivalent of a lunar landing. Passes into space are among the best non-goals for the same reasons the Apollo missions are so inspiring. They require vision, attention to detail, and a desire to break through lines and boundaries to connect with unexplored aspects of existence. They require the best of both skills and energies. They're also the type of non-goal that is most like the holiest of American sports holies: the touchdown pass.

Let's take a look at one excellent example of the pass into space: a stratosphere-piercing through ball from France's mercurial midfielder Paul Pogba during 2021's 2020 Euro Cup (the tournament was delayed a year due to the COVID-19 pandemic but they kept the name). Pogba is probably too tall and inconsistently excellent to be an astronaut, but when the stars align, his timing, precision, and technical expertise are on par with the best to ever wear a flight suit.

In this non-goal, Pogba is launching a counter

A pass into space is the soccer equivalent of a perfectly-executed Apollo mission.

attack against Switzerland. As the ball bounces his way near the center of the field, he hopes to quickly advance his team with a defense-stretching pass down the flank to his teammate, Marcus Thuram. In an instant, he determines the trajectory of the ricocheting ball, takes two quick steps backward, and adjusts his body position to match the path of the ball, then steps into the pass making sure to keep his foot over the top of the ball so that it doesn't end up on Jupiter. With this effort, he can send the ball into the path of his speedier teammates—quickly breaking into the attacking zone of the field before the opposing defense has a chance to prepare. It's exactly what Kennedy had hoped to do to his Soviet rivals—get out ahead of the game as quickly and definitively as possible. Pogba's perfectly placed pass out wide gives France an edge and puts them in a good position, even though the attack eventually fizzles out.

As you might know, the Apollo spacecraft had three parts: the command module that housed the pilots, the service module that propelled the craft, and the lunar module built to land softly on the surface of the moon. Pogba's pass essentially has the same elements:

- His brain is the command module, navigating space and making decisions on where to position his body to send his pass.

- His right foot is the service module, propelling the ball with the right speed, loft and backspin to land directly in the path of Thuram at the perfect moment.

- The ball is the lunar module, hurtling

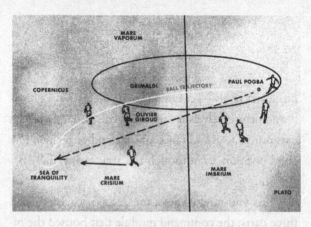

Pogba's pass into space.

toward the surface and setting down at Tranquility Base: the feet of his teammate. Neil Armstrong couldn't have done it better.

- As a bonus, we've even got a Buzz Aldrin on this mission: French striker Olivier Giroud, who arrives on the scene 15 minutes late, thereby missing out on the glory of Pogba's setup.

America's space program advanced humanity's understanding of our world and worlds beyond, while laying the groundwork for technologies that would change our lives forever. Earthlings were able to follow this progress in entirely new ways, with updates on the international space race available to a worldwide audience, culminating in the live television broadcast of humans walking on the moon. A non-goal pass like Pogba's is a much smaller feat, but still significant. Viewed by millions of people all over the globe, igniting the imaginations of soccer fans, and inspiring players to dream about what's possible on the field, each non-goal mission drives the soccer world forward, inching toward ever bigger moments on the world stage.

While we're on the topic of space, we should discuss one of the greatest passtronauts (had to do it) of all time, Andres Iniesta. Never have so many passes been sent into space with the majesty and precision of those launched from the Iniesta launchpad. A non-goal factory for FC Barcelona between 2004 and 2018, Iniesta actually scored two of the most famous goals of the last twenty years: a perfectly struck and guided missile versus Chelsea FC in a controversial Champions League semi-final in 2009, and the game-winning strike in the 2010 World Cup Final that brought Spain their first FIFA trophy.

But while those two goals will live at the top of Iniesta's resumé forever, his greatest contributions to the game regularly came in the form of non-goals.

Spain's living space program, Andres Iniesta.

Iniesta was a small, physically unimposing player, but he was a master of keeping the ball at his feet under pressure. His inventiveness with the ball was bettered only by his vision as a passer. Iniesta's Barcelona were known for their possession of the ball—it wasn't unusual for his team to have the ball 75–80% of the game—but Iniesta consistently created incisions through the opponent's defensive lines and onto the feet of his strikers, ensuring that after long passages of meandering possession Barcelona would find a way to score in the end. Fusing vision, composure, and skills of the highest order, Iniesta was the archetypal non-goal creator. A typical Iniesta passage of play might feature several non-goals strung together—deploying a magical first-touch to corral the ball, nimbly maneuvering around a defender or three with his patented "croqueta" technique, playing a quick one-two with another midfielder to confound the defense, and finally playing a ball into space for an open striker to run onto. Iniesta could package an entire Apollo mission into a six-second passage of play, several times a game, every game of the year. American Jerry Ross went into space seven times (a record) and Iniesta was equally important to his club and his country, winning an absurd number of trophies, exploring new galaxies on the field, and gaining praise from then-Barcelona manager Pep Guardiola for his "mastery of the relationship between space and time." While he may never have visited the moon, it was in doing the other things that made Iniesta a human space program.

OFFSIDE IS CHEATING:
Your guide to soccer's most misunderstood rule.

The offside rule was created to prevent "cherry picking," or the practice of standing around in front of the opponent's goal waiting for a chance to go 1-on-1 with the keeper. The rule is simple but relative, and this relativity has been known to cause confusion in those accustomed to sports rules of the absolute variety.

A PLAYER IS OFFSIDE WHEN:

- They are closer to the opponents' goal than both the ball and two opponents
- The player is directly involved in the play

When attempting to determine whether or not a player is offside, ask yourself: *where was the player when the ball was last touched by a teammate?* Was the player hoping to get out in front of the defense for an easy, devious, unguarded shot on goal? Or was the player keeping level with the penultimate opponent, minding his own business and following the rules?

Additional context: being in an offside position was originally called "sneaking," and anything called "sneaking" is likely to be illegal or, at best, frowned upon. Pro tip: Sneaky soccer players are "offside," not "offsides." Save the plural form for American football.

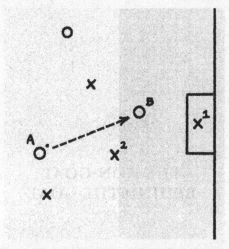

Sneaky Player B is offside when the ball is passed.

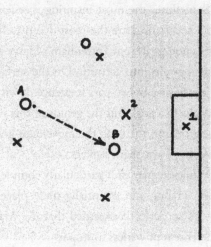

Player B is onside.

THE NON-GOAL
BEHIND THE GOAL

Sometimes the most inspiring moments you'll see on a soccer field are the most deceptively simple. Take this non-goal from Tottenham's Harry Kane and Son Heung-min into account. On the surface, we've got a pretty simple two-pass sequence down the field that results in a goal. But the genius of this play is the non-goal behind the goal: the movement and timing between the Tottenham strikers.

While the play isn't particularly complex—Kane and Son Heung-min essentially trade places on the field—it's so perfectly executed that the Manchester City defense is powerless to stop it.

Kane begins the play as Tottenham's most forward player, but as his teammate Ben Davies regains

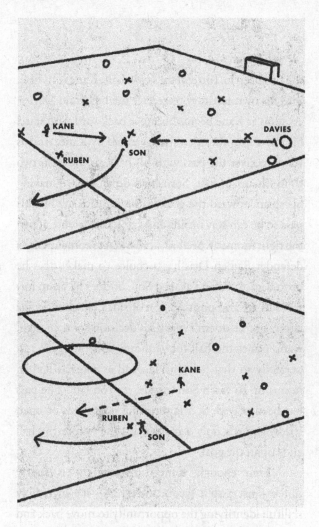

Kane and Son's inventive movement generate the non-goal behind the goal.

the ball deep in Tottenham's own half, Kane runs back into his own territory to receive the ball from Davies. As soon as Kane begins his move backward, Son starts his move into the open space vacated by Kane. And as Kane receives the pass with his back to the goal, two things happen: first, Son slows down before making his sprint toward the goal,waiting until Kane hits his pass so he can stay onside and catch the defense at just the right moment. Second, at this exact moment City's defender Ruben Dias has a choice to make: does he drop back to defend against Son, or does he jump forward to try and position Son offside? He chooses the latter, but he doesn't make his decision soon enough. Kane passes the ball forward and Son times his run perfectly so that he's onside. And as soon as Ruben jumps up to catch Son offside, it's too late. The pass has been played, Son is sprinting into yards of open space, and it's only a matter of time before the ball ends up in the goal.

Even though Kane's involvement is pretty quick—just a split second of a pass—it's incredibly skillful; identifying the opportunity to move back and receive the pass, playing a first-time pass with his weaker left foot as a defender closes him down, and hitting the pass with exactly the right amount of power and accuracy to put Son into free space are all best-in-class ideas and skills. Son is equally responsible, as he made the run knowing that Kane would look to release him as soon as Kane got the ball, timing it perfectly.

On the other side of the ball, I assume Manchester City manager Pep Guardiola is upset about three things:

- No pressure on the first passer. Ben Davies has too much time and space to make an incisive pass to Harry Kane.

- City's defense is slow in closing down Kane. He has enough space and freedom to deliver his pass to Son without much of a challenge from the defenders.

- Ruben's decision to catch Son offside comes too slowly. He could have made a safer decision to move backward and defend instead of jumping up.

Son's signature celebration.

While Guardiola might not be too happy, this is a pretty terrific moment for non-goal fans. A simple idea perfectly executed, beautiful team play, and craftsmanship—what a time to be alive.

MISE EN PLACE

Mise en place is a French culinary phrase, expressing the idea that a chef should have all of their ingredients prepared and ready to use before cooking begins. Mise en place translates roughly to "everything in place," and is a guiding principle used by world-renowned chefs and home cooks in kitchens all over the world. If you've ever started cooking dinner only to realize that the next step calls for a dozen peeled and sliced garlic cloves that you haven't prepared, you've felt the pain of life without mise en place. A chef looking for the most streamlined and stress-free cooking experience will make sure all of their onions have been chopped, their carrots have been peeled, and everything is in front of them before the stove clicks into ignition.

It's unclear whether Julia Child supported Paris St. Germain or Olympique Lyonnais, based in the culinary capital of France.

In America, mise en place has a patron saint: Julia Child. The lanky, late-blooming, muppet-sounding chef, author, and TV cooking show host was trained in the French culinary tradition while living in Paris with her husband who was on assignment with the U.S. State Department. Child is an icon, and you're probably familiar with her legacy as the person who made high-brow European cooking methods accessible to American home cooks. Along with boeuf bourguignon, sole meunière, and proper omelet technique, Child introduced the idea of mise en place to home cooks more familiar with chicken casseroles than coq au vin. With mise en place, cooking could be an adventure without becoming a disaster. Organization, vision, and preparation could help you stay sane while preparing dinner for hungry, ungrateful kids or a dinner party of neighborhood VIPs—proving that a little foresight and preparedness can unlock a highly creative cooking experience.

Which brings us back to the soccer field. There is a select group of players who believe in the power of mise en place, constantly looking for new ingredients and combining them in innovative ways. These players rely on reading the recipe in advance, understanding the raw materials in front of them, and making split-second improvisations when the steak is ready before the potatoes and the *au poivre* needs a bit more poivre. These are highly skilled players, often found roaming midfields weeknights, deep into the knockout stages of upper echelon European tournaments. Responsible for orchestrating their team's attacking play, these players know the menu by heart and they're constantly experimenting with techniques that give

*Luka Modric, the Thomas Keller of
European soccer.*

their teams an edge. While they're all cooking different kinds of food, one thing they've got in common is their unique ability to take stock of the ingredients in front of them, quickly prepare the dish in their mind, and craft it to perfection under the glow of the Champions League heat lamps.

While we don't know if Luka Modric has read Child's *Mastering the Art of French Cooking*, he's definitely practicing the art of mise en place. Few players are better at getting the ball from defense to attack in just one touch, and it's vital for him to understand what's happening on the field around him in order to play first-time passes forward to attacking players. At any given time, Modric is scanning the field to see where his teammates are. He's looking forward and back, across the field, and checking the movement of the defense at the same time. Because Modric is playing in the center of the field, his cooking surface surrounds him in 360 degrees, with his ingredients in constant motion. Without scanning the field, he'd be flying blind, improvising a meal without any idea what he's got in the fridge. But by regularly looking around the field he's snapping mental photos of the scene around him, ready to get the ball where it needs to be, and making use of seasonal ingredients supplied in the mid-season transfer window. These passes might move down the field toward the opposing team's goal or back into safer territory to re-start his team's attack—whatever the occasion calls for. Midfielders like Modric create this kind of non-goal fairly often during a game by playing a pass to the right player at the right time, and if you look closely you'll see many actual goals start with the mise en place of a well-prepared midfielder.

Modric is a well-known non-goal culinary master. Having won the Champions League multiple times with Real Madrid, played in the World Cup final with Croatia, and been awarded the Ballon d'Or as Europe's best player for the 2018 season, he's essentially the Thomas Keller of world soccer. Somewhat lesser known, playing on a smaller stage for Spain's Villareal (also known as "The Yellow Submarine" due to their all-yellow uniforms), is Dani Parejo. Parejo generally occupies a deeper spot on the field just in front of his defenders, but he's also a master of understanding the scene around him by constantly scanning the field. Parejo and Villareal gained a bit of notoriety by punching above their weight and reaching the semi-finals of the Champions League in the spring of 2022 by playing well-organized defense and finishing clinically on the counter attack. Teams employing this strategy often rely on a player like Parejo to transition play from defense to attack with a quick outlet pass from the center of the field. In the example pictured here, you'll see Parejo run back to receive a pass from his own keeper and then instantly play the ball out wide to an advanced winger with one touch of the ball. He scans the field several times to put his mise en place in

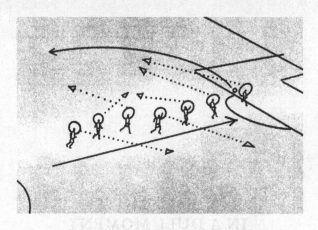

*As he moves toward his own goal, Dani Parejo
scans the field around him, eventually playing a
perfect pass forward into open space.*

order and with one strike of the ball he's whipped up
a tasty non-goal to the delight of millions of hungry
viewers.

Julia Child once said, "The more you know, the
more you can create. There's no end to imagination
in the kitchen." As so many creative geniuses know,
the key to unlocking creativity is often just the right
amount of structure. By applying mise en place in
the kitchen and on the soccer field, chefs, cooks and
box-to-box midfielders learn to take stock of what's in
front of them before they create, setting the table for a
rich feast of ingeniously crafted meals and non-goals.

A BOLD MOVE
IN A DULL MOMENT

November, 1775: Boston, Massachusetts. American general and bookstore owner Henry Knox leads a select group of soldiers through 300 miles of rough, snow-covered terrain to bring badly needed cannons south from Fort Ticonderoga to the surrounding hills. The Americans are desperate to expel British troops from Boston, where the redcoats had hunkered down earlier in the year, and fortifying Dorchester Heights outside of the city would give the Americans the advantage they needed to drive the British out. Knox, who is not trained as a soldier but has studied military strategy from the shelves of bookstores he's worked in for years (he left school to support his family at the age of nine after his father's death), commands his expedition as they move 60 tons of artillery through ridiculously impassable terrain using an inventive combination of boats, sleds, and oxen, crossing frozen rivers, swamps, and forests to strengthen America's position in Dorchester Heights.

This was an unconventional but highly successful move. Revolutionary War winters were generally not times of great troop activity, with armies preferring to make camp and endure freezing temperatures and limited supplies without adding battle to their list of challenges. Some winters, like that of 1780, were so cold that many troops were on the verge of starvation, which makes Knox's three-month run to Ticonderoga and back (also known as the "noble train of artillery") all the more exceptional—big, bold moves during the winter months of the Revolutionary War were rare. While most of the army waited out the weather, Knox fought the New England winter. After retrieving the cannons from Ticonderoga, Knox and company repeatedly beat the season at its own game—constructing bespoke sleds that carried the artillery over the heavy snow (over two feet were reported on Christmas Day) and even adding water on top of a freezing river to accelerate the thickening process.

Once Knox returned with the artillery, the Americans began their secret fortification. Overnight, as another Continental Army base fired on the British occupation in Boston, American soldiers lugged Knox's cannons to the tops of Dorchester Heights. In the morning, stunned British General William Howe declared, "My God, these fellows have done more work in one night than I could make my army do in three months." Seeing the improved position of the Americans and their reinforced artillery, the British immediately retreated and evacuated Boston without firing a single shot.

Almost 250 years later, the British are still vulnerable to a bold move during a dull moment, even if the attacks are coming from their own countrymen on a soccer field. On a late-spring day in 2022, another band of redcoats, similarly looking to hang on to an era of global domination while away from home, face a rag-tag group of under-funded and seemingly over-matched troops. Manchester United, one of the most successful European teams in the last 50 years, face little Brighton Hove Albion, with United expecting to win on Brighton's home turf. But in the 14th minute Brighton summons their own noble train of artillery,

Manchester United goalkeeper David de Gea.

using the reliably quiet moment of a throw-in to better their position and eventually strike through United's unassuming defense.

Throw-ins: there's probably not a less exciting moment in a soccer game. The ball rolls out of bounds, the player closest to the sideline saunters over to the ball, walks back up the line, stands around for a bit looking for open feet to throw to, and then tosses the ball back into play. Sometimes the ball ends up out of bounds again and the routine is repeated. But for smaller teams like Brighton looking for any possible edge against perennial powers like Manchester United, throw-ins are an opportunity to fortify their armies and prepare for a bold move. Known for his unconventional coaching methods, Brighton manager Graham Potter led Brighton into this battle in the image of George Washington himself: no tactic was left unturned and the element of surprise was often utilized (for example, striking while the enemy slept was a classic Washington tactic, used over and over again as the Americans flustered and frustrated the British).

After listlessly marching through the first 13 minutes of the game, United eventually misplace a pass that rolls out past the sideline. Brighton cunningly take their time retrieving the ball, and, as United uses the moment to catch their breath, the Brighton midfield advances downfield to take better position. An astute viewer will even notice Potter gesture his players forward with a subtle pushing motion toward the United goal. The throw comes in, and as the ball bounces off of a United defender's head, Brighton midfielder Moisés Caicedo advances 20 yards to win the ball back and initiate Brighton's attack. United are slow to react, and before they're able to organize their defense Brighton has crossed the ball into United's box. United manage

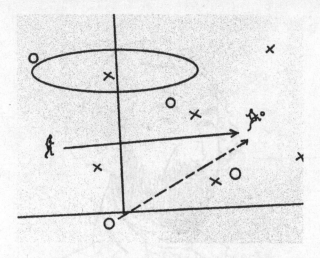

Caicedo's movement gives Brighton a better position
from the throw-in.

to clear the ball away, but Brighton continue their forward pressure. Caicedo again advances into a position just outside of the United penalty area, takes control of the ricocheting ball, and fires it into the goal from the top of Dorchester Heights. The TV replay focuses on the goal, of course, and the commentators turn their attention to narrative: it's Caicedo's first goal for the team, the mighty United have fallen from grace, et cetera. But it's another non-goal before the goal that makes the play really interesting. It's Brighton's bold movement during the dark night of the throw-in that gives them the advantage, and it's their re-positioning during a sleepy passage of play that puts Caicedo in

*Brighton manager Graham Potter hatching his
next Washingtonian scheme.*

position to strike. The goal itself is OK—it's an accurately hit ball into the low corner—but Potter's Knox-like expedition is the best part of the play. And, like the noble train of artillery, Caicedo's bold offensive works out well for the scrappy underdogs. Like true revolutionaries, Brighton continued their Washingtonian attacks and ran United out of town, the redcoats waving the white flag without even mustering a strike of their own. The final score: Brighton 4, United 0.

LETTING IT BE:
THE BEATLES, PELÉ, AND
THE ART OF RESTRAINT

In the spring of 1969, The Beatles got together to get back to basics. After several years of increasingly complex recording processes, and increasingly complex personal and creative relationships, the band was hoping to recapture the magic of their early years: four incredibly talented guys playing music in a room together, without dense layers of studio polish complicating their output.

Many of us know this story, especially if you've seen the Peter Jackson film, *Get Back*, documenting the recording of what would eventually become their album, *Let It Be*. In that moment, The Beatles were at the height of their fame and success, with as much creative potential as any rock band in history. With un-

precedented financial resources and the gravity to sum-
mon any musical talent to collaborate on the project,
the Fab Four could have made any record they wanted.
But instead of opting for the multi-tracked intricacy of
their recent records, the question they decided to ask
was: what happens if we just let it be?

One year later, over 5,000 miles away in Gua-
dalajara, Mexico, something similar happened on a
soccer field, in the semi-finals of the 1970 World Cup.
Brazil's Pelé, one the greatest attacking players in history, made a run down the center field. His compatriot
Tostão looked up and played a ball into the space in
front of Pelé, leading him directly in front of goal. The
opposing goalkeeper, Uruguay's Ladislao Mazurkiewicz, sprinted out to meet Pelé, hoping to get a foot
on the ball before Pelé could score. What happened
next has been called "the greatest goal never scored,"
making it perhaps the world's greatest-ever non-goal.
It was a play so inventive, so incredible, so skillful that
only a master could produce it—a non-goal so good it
even has its own Wikipedia entry.

With a perfect pass placed in front of him, and
only the keeper to stop him, on the biggest stage imaginable, Pelé, perhaps the most talented soccer player of

*The 1970 Brazilian World Cup team: Tostão, Pelé, Jairzin-
ho and Carlos Alberto Torres (clockwise, from top left).*

all-time, decided *not to touch* the ball. To let the ball roll
past him and the keeper while everyone in the stadium
(including Mazurkiewicz) expected Pelé to shoot. To
let it be.

As the ball rolled past Mazurkiewicz, who was
now completely exposed several yards out of his box,
Pelé sprinted forward to retrieve the ball and quickly
shoot before the keeper could get back into position.
Although he got to the ball with what appeared to be

enough time and space to hit an accurate shot on goal, somehow the ball bounced wide of the post and out of bounds. Maybe the sight of a Uruguayan defender covering the goal threw Pelé off, maybe he was as surprised as anybody that his daring non-touch had worked. But somehow this inventive, counterintuitive play didn't result in a goal that would have certainly been one of the greatest ever scored in the World Cup, and thereby the history of the world.

How could it be that Pelé, with such incredible talent and experience, playing with the best team in the world, would decide to *not kick* the ball? Was it the same instinct that The Beatles had to eschew the studio wizardry of the era for an unexpectedly lighter production touch? How did these icons of creativity know that in the biggest moments, sometimes giving up control can set you free? Soccer and sports in general are often defined by what a player does with the ball. Dribbling, passing, even defending are built on the idea of taking action with the ball. It's this element of surprising inaction that makes what's known in soccer as a "dummy" so interesting: a player lets the ball play past them when the world expects them to take a touch, pass, or shoot, subverting the expectations of

A dummy in action. Player A lets the ball roll past him to Player B, who shoots on goal. Defenders C and D were drawn in by the dummy and are now exposed.

opponents and viewers. Dummies work so well because they draw defensive attention to a player that appears likely to take action on the ball. A good dummy forces a reaction by the opposing team that pulls them out of position, or it requires an adjustment that leaves them vulnerable to an ensuing attack. At its most direct a dummy can lead to a goal right away, if the player performing the dummy draws attention while letting the ball roll to a teammate with a clear, undefended shot. Indirectly, dummies can lead to a transition of play from one part of the field to another that stretches the defense and makes their job harder. In the context of an entire game, a well-executed dummy can make defensive players hesitant to apply the same amount of pressure when a player is receiving the ball later on. Whether the impact of a successful dummy is seen immediately or cumulatively throughout a game, it's one of the most fun and unique non-goals to behold.

Most Beatles fans would agree that *Let It Be* is not the group's best record. There are moments of excellence like "Get Back," "I've Got a Feeling," or the title track, but there are also half-finished and ill-conceived songs that make the record a bit of a let-down from The Beatles' incredibly high standards. But even though it's not their most highly-regarded album, it contains moments that are just as legendary as anything the group ever did: the audacity to strip their sound back to its essentials, the spontaneity to perform a live show on the rooftop of their studio in the middle of the day, the culmination of inner turmoil that launched them all into their own individual pursuits. It's precisely their willingness to take their hands off of the process that makes *Let It Be* so iconic, just as it's Pelé's instinct to let the ball roll that makes this non-goal so audacious and memorable. It's a rare moment of inaction that rivals any moment of action on the soccer field.

The Beatles went back into the studio for one more record after *Let It Be*, and the resultant *Abbey Road* was full of the kind of action we love from the band. Multi-tracked vocal harmonies and dense layers of traditional and experimental musical sounds were a big part of The Beatles' final record together (George Harrison wheeled his own custom-made Moog synthesizer into the studio for the sessions), just as Pelé went on to take plenty of action with the ball, winning the 1970 World Cup and scoring against Italy in the final, which would be his last. Famed for their industry as much as their quality in the early years of their careers, it's interesting that these famous moments of inaction took place in the final stages of both The Beatles' and Pelé's creative journeys. Could the early Beatles, playing several shows each night in the nightclubs of Hamburg and putting maximum effort into their studio work, imagine taking their foot off the gas to rediscover their creative magic? And could Pelé, the youngest person to ever play in a World Cup Final at

*Paul McCartney claims to support Liverpool and
Everton "equally" and is obviously lying.*

17, imagine that every time he touched the ball he'd set
the stage for the most famous non-touch in the history of the game? Dummies only work when defenders
have an expectation that the offensive player will actually play the ball, which is why dummies from the
most renowned creative minds come at such a surprise
and make such a lasting impression. Only through
such prodigious action could a surprising moment of
inaction become so legendary.

THE MAZE, THE MINOTAUR, AND THE MILAN MIDFIELDER

According to ancient Greek legend, a half-man, half-bull creature called the Minotaur murderously devoured the seven most courageous young men and the seven most beautiful maidens from a rival kingdom every seven years. Living on the island of Crete, the Minotaur resided in an enormous labyrinth built by the brilliant craftsman Daedalus, who designed it to confine the flesh-eating beast. Escape was impossible, for the Minotaur as well as his victims. The maze was so well designed that even Daedelus had a difficult time getting out once it was completed, and when unfortunate young folks were dropped into the maze it was only a matter of time before the Minotaur found them and consumed them.

I sometimes wonder, as I'm sure you do, what trying to escape this maze felt like to the men and maidens looking for a way out. Was it like the never-ending pressure of a Jurgen Klopp-esque German gegenpress[1]—relentless and suffocating? Or was it more like the Sisyphean task of trying to chip away at a Jose Mourinho-style bus parking[2], making pass after pass fully knowing you're more likely to find yourself conceding a goal on the counter-attack than making your own breakthrough?

1. Liverpool Manager Jurgen Klopp is known for an intense style of defense, known as a gegenpress. Similar to a full-court press in basketball, this plan requires all players to apply intense defensive pressure high up the field, wreaking havoc on teams without the skills to pass and dribble themselves free of the suffocating pressure.
2. Some teams choose to place their entire team in their own half, fortifying the area in front of their own goal and absorbing attacks in the hopes of eventually regaining possession and quickly striking on a counter-attack. Almost like a self-imposed siege, this tactic has come to be known as "parking the bus," implying that the team's plans amount to nothing more than driving the team bus onto the field and placing it in front of their own goal. Often effective at keeping the ball out of the goal, this plan is detested by fans due to its cynical nature and the low-scoring affairs it often produces. Coach Jose Mounrinho is one well-known devotee of this tactic.

Theseus in the AC Milan midfield.

Greek mythology is full of tales like that of the Minotaur, with seemingly unbeatable foes posing seemingly insurmountable challenges. But as is the case in many of these stories, defeating the Minotaur required two things: a hero and a plan. In the story of the Minotaur, a young hero named Theseus arrived in the winter transfer window to put an end to the carnage caused by the Minotaur. Theseus was celebrated for being a more sophisticated, better-read version of fellow legend Heracles and was beloved by the people of Athens for his brainy heroics. Known for his incredible strength, Heracles was the superhero of superheroes, able to overcome any obstacle by sheer power alone. Theseus on the other hand was as crafty and resourceful as he was strong. As historian Edith Hamilton puts it, Theseus was "a man of great intellect as well as great bodily strength. It was natural that the Athenians should have such a hero, because they valued thought and ideas, as no other part of the country did."

With the help of a local youth academy member named Ariadne, Theseus entered the maze with two tools: a sword and a ball of yarn. Theseus used the yarn to make a map of the maze by dragging it behind him as he made his way through. If he ran into a dead end he'd simply follow his yarn back and find another way, like a more successful Hansel and Gretel. But as brilliant as Theseus was, the plan to defeat the Minotaur wasn't his. A plan so crafty could only come from the architect himself: Daedalus. When Daedalus saw that his friend Ariadne had fallen in love with Theseus he gave her the plan so that she could give it to Theseus. Upon reaching the end of the maze, Theseus surprised the Minotaur and easily slew it with his sword, in one of the most anticlimactic final boss battles in Greek

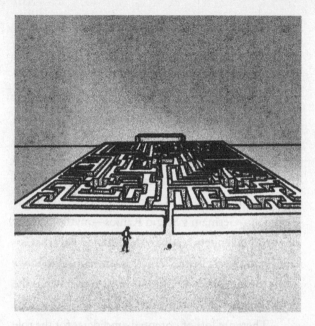

Finding a way through an aggressive or densely packed defense is an eternal human struggle. Some heroes do it better than others.

mythology. Navigating the maze might have been tedious. It may have required balling up the yarn and starting over from the beginning more than once, but getting through an expertly crafted maze is rarely done on the first try. Beating the maze was the tough part. Defeating the Minotaur just required a well-timed strike.

In the present day, courageous teams of young men and maidens fail to find a way through mazes constructed by tactical craftsmen like Atletico Madrid manager Diego Simeone or Chelsea's Thomas Tuchel. On weekends between August and June, labyrinths created by defensive-minded managers stifle teams packed with elite attacking talent. And inside of these mazes lie Minotaurs like Liverpool's Virgil Van Dijk or Paris Saint-Germain's Sergio Ramos—mythologically powerful defenders ready to devour attackers that aren't up to the challenge. Where is *our* hero, who is *our* Theseus, and who's got the ball of yarn to unwind the defensive maze set before him?

There are lots of potential candidates for the role of legendary maze-breaker Theseus: the speedy Frenchman Kylian Mbappé, the skillful Portuguese Bruno Fernandes, even the long-range airborne assault of Brazilian goalkeeper Ederson could find the way through a deviously devised maze. But to find our Theseus we'll begin with a recent legend of Mediterranean lands: Italy's Andrea Pirlo. Seemingly blessed with few physical gifts—not speedy like contemporary Italian midfielder Barella, nor with the bulldog-like obstinance of his midfield partner Gennaro Gattuso—Pirlo's intellect helped him navigate a variety of mazes throughout his career, roaming stadiums in the north of Italy with an urgency better suited for a game of bacci than the soccer field. But underneath this mild-mannered exterior lay a master maze-breaker. Pirlo's ability to cut through defenses with just one or two passes was sublime, and his expertise in beginning or re-starting an attack from deep in his own half was second-to-none. Before you can kill the Minotaur you have to find him, and Pirlo's journey to the center of the maze would often uncover non-goals around every corner. Whether in the form of visionary 30-yard passes over the maze walls, subtle changes of pace or direction that left eager defenders guessing, or well-timed backward passes to escape oncoming Minotaurs, Pirlo's non-goal output was perpetual, rising every morning like Homer's rosy fingers of the dawn.

Playing the midfield role known as the "regista," or "director" in Italian soccer vernacular, Pirlo occupied the space just in front of his defense. From this vantage point he could begin his team's attack with every option in front of him—almost like having a top-down view of the maze. He seemed to always have his ball of yarn at the ready, and when his team might find itself at a dead end he'd be there to wind up the yarn, bring them back to the starting point and find another

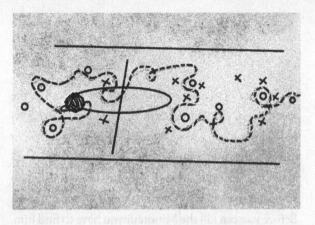

*Pirlo's ball of yarn unspools as it's passed and
dribbled through the defense.*

way through—always as cool as the captain of a yacht
on calm Mediterranean waters. This was our hero's
plan: to never panic, to never give in to the pressure of
a labyrinth's walls closing in, and to always be ready to
follow the yarn back to the beginning and start again.
He would do this relentlessly until finally, as if aided
by the gods, his team found itself in front of the goal,
maze broken, ready to slay the unsuspecting Minotaur
with the most anticlimactic of tap-ins.

Unlike other sports, possession in soccer is not
finite. It's not limited to 24 seconds or 4 downs. A
soccer team could hang onto the ball for the entire 90
minutes, in theory, and would face no penalization
or discipline from the officials. An attack can begin,
flow down the field, move backward in retreat, begin

from a new point, shift again, eventually find a way through, or dissolve altogether. This is why starting over is such an important idea in soccer. Retracing your steps and beginning again is not a concept friendly to American sports. Basketball is a sport of constant forward motion–going backward is literally illegal if a team takes the ball back across the halfcourt line once they've crossed it. In American football, the odds of success grow slimmer the more yards a team retreats into their own territory. But in soccer, you can't always go forward. Mazes constructed by brilliant managers, the Deadali of today, limit forward progress. Minotaur-like defenders converge on the ball. In soccer, winding up your ball of yarn is not a sign of weakness, it's heroic.

After Italy's World Cup win in 2006, the team slowly came unwound—exiting the 2010 and 2014 World Cup in the group stages, then failing to even qualify in 2018. Italy needed to start over. Rebuilding with a new group of talented young players, Italy won the 2020 European Cup in 2021, led again by a new regista, Jorginho. Born in Brazil but with Italian citizenship, Jorginho started playing professionally in Italy at 15, eventually finding his way to London's

Chelsea FC. In our mythology Jorginho picks up where Pirlo left off. Quicker, with instincts that pull him forward into attacking positions more often than Pirlo, you might see him starting an attack near midfield and surfacing again just outside his opponent's box to take a shot on goal or play a short diagonal ball to an open striker. Like Theseus, you'll see him looking for ways through, around, and over the maze. He's constantly following the yarn to pull the team forward or back—whatever is necessary to find an open passage. At any moment, Jorginho might provide a variety of non-goals, from a defense-splitting pass into the 18-yard box, to an attack-switching pivot pass from a dead end into an open passage, to a sly body fake that throws a defender off balance. Is Jorginho the future, or an echo from the past? Is he a new kind of hero, or just the newest telling of a very old story?

Pirlo was a once-in-a-generation player. Winner of six Italian Serie A titles, two Champions League titles, and the World Cup trophy in 2006, Pirlo was one of the most prolific non-goal creators of the aughts. Born just a thousand miles from the Athenian home of Theseus, the small, not particularly fast or strong Andrea Pirlo became the non-goal creating heir to the ancient Greek hero because he wasn't afraid to start over. But whether we watch Pirlo, Jorginho, or new players to come, a regista's faith in the plan, and their expertise in executing it, is the key to defeating the most mythic of challenges.

THE 2022
NON-GOAL OF THE YEAR

Luis Diaz is a Colombian-born striker currently electrifying European soccer fields from Madrid to the banks of Liverpool's River Mersey. Signed by Liverpool FC seemingly in the middle of a dark and stormy night, Diaz's play has been similar to his acquisition—blindingly quick, indelibly brilliant, and immediately impactful.

Diaz was a mid-season pickup. The winter transfer window is usually reserved for desperate attempts to save a season, with teams often overpaying for overcooked or overrated players past their prime or unlikely to ever experience one, hoping for a boost to the top of the league or, more desperately, to avoid relegation to a lower league the following year. The Diaz

A lightning strike is nearly as fast and deadly as a Luis Diaz counter-attack.

signing was something else. In the few short months he has been with Liverpool he's been unquestionably successful. Illuminating the left side of the field, Diaz's speed and movement on and off the ball lights up The Reds' attack—most evidently when he appears as a substitute late in the game, kicking in like a backup generator to power Liverpool's offense during a storm.

Many players run fast. What sets Diaz apart is his direct relationship with calamity. He is an emergency. Every touch of the ball is potentially dangerous, every run spells trouble for the defense. Diaz is the fork in the microwave—a rattling, spinning, sparking crisis you only hope you can get to before your kitchen needs remodeling. If you were lucky enough to see Diaz play in the few months since he's joined Liverpool, you'll have seen the electricity he brings to the field. At any moment, he's able to conjure first touches that nobody else saw coming, footwork that only he can keep up with, and vision to include teammates at the right moment.

So it shouldn't be a surprise that the best non-goal of the year contains all three of these elements in one play: about 4 seconds of non-goal ecstasy during England's Carabao Cup Final against Chelsea (The Carabao Cup is one of the more baffling season-long tournaments in Europe, essentially a knockout tournament featuring teams from England's top four professional leagues). Not only was the final an incredibly entertaining 0-0 draw, eventually won by Liverpool on penalties, it was a non-goal smorgasbord, and living proof of soccer's redeeming entertainment value with or without goals. Between outstanding individual and team efforts, and excellent goalkeeping and defending, the Carabao Cup Final had it all for the non-goal fan, and moments like this Diaz non-goal were what made it so special.

Right around the 74th minute, Diaz received a long pass down the sideline from teammate Andrew Roberstson. As the pass traveled down the line toward Diaz, he knew he'd be under pressure from Chelsea's Reece James, quickly approaching from behind and hoping to limit the time Diaz had to make a decision on the ball. A more conservative player might quickly pass the ball back where it came from, or hold and shield for a moment while he found an option, but not Diaz. He knew that the pressure being applied by James would be his escape route. If he could just flick the ball up and over James, which he did marvelously, he could use James' own momentum against him in one of the best Judo moves you'll see on a soccer field. As he used his back foot to skillfully flip the rolling ball up into the air, he also gave it just the right forward spin to keep the ball traveling in the same direction toward Chelsea's goal. Diaz did a quick swim move

Opposite: A step-by-step reenactment of the
2022 Non-Goal of the Year.

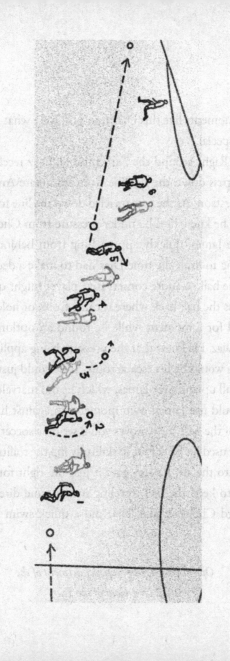

to get his body past James while the ball arced over the defender's shoulder, and James was beaten. This required defender Trevoh Chalobah to slide over and try to cover. Leaving James behind him, Diaz kept his head up and the play in front of him. At the same time he noticed Chalobah attempting to close him down, he saw his teammate Sadio Mane run into free space down the line. Knowing that he wanted to get the ball to Mane but wanting to make sure Mane had as much space as possible, he froze Chalobah with a quick look to the middle of the field. Diaz held this look to his right as he passed the ball to his left, ensuring Chalobah wouldn't be able to get a foot on his pass to Mane and enshrining this play into non-goal history.

Eventually Liverpool's attack dissolved but the non-goal was achieved. This play epitomizes what we love about non-goals: the ingenious creativity moving from Diaz's brain to his feet in microseconds, the skilled craftsmanship honed over decades of work, and the vision required to make those 4 seconds so delightful are what we love to celebrate. And this was just one of several Diaz created in that game alone, which was full of non-goals. These moments aren't recorded in the score sheet and they likely won't make the highlight reel, but they're what make soccer such a rich and enduring spectacle. Congratulations to Luis Diaz on winning the first-ever Non-Goal of the Year for 2022 and thank you for making 2021–2022 such a wonderful season.

THE FIRST WAVE

The ball starts with the American goalkeeper. Short passes between his center backs and deep-lying midfielder don't expose any gaps in the defense, so the ball goes back to the keeper. He's on the edge of his own goal line now, but he's not obviously panicked as the defense applies pressure on him. More patient, short passes are played and the ball eventually finds its way out wide to the fullback. Another pass is played to a winger who has come back into his own half to help, but it's a dead end. The ball goes all the way back to the goalkeeper again. The defense applies more pressure. American fans in the stadium express an uneasy tension, or is it boredom? Suddenly a long ball is played to a striker who has retreated from the center circle. This

Can Christian Pulisic deliver a masterpiece in 2022?

opens things up a bit. The striker flicks the ball up into the air, into the path of another attacker—America's biggest star, Christian Pulisic—who rushes forward to receive it. Pulisic controls the ball with his chest and brings it forward at pace.

The Americans are now in their opponents' half of the field with lots of open space at their disposal. A winger started making a run forward a moment ago and now Pulisic makes a pass out in front of the speedy guy, 25 yards from the opposition's goal. Now with a numerical advantage, the Americans push further forward, as the winger plays a perfectly timed pass into the path of the striker who is now directly in front of the goal at the end of a 50-yard sprint. He shoots. Blocked.

On paper it reads like a smooth and fluidly executed attack. To behold, it was wobbly, like a baby giraffe taking its first steps, or an IKEA table hastily assembled in a dorm room. But in the space of 30 seconds, the ball was moved patiently, if at times awkwardly, from one end of the field to the other, and at the end of a string of 13 uninterrupted passes, a shot was taken. A good shot, from a good location that forced a good save. This is what the English might call "good football." It's the kind of play you'll see from the best teams in the world—Manchester City, Liverpool, Bayern Munich—and it's very difficult to do. Up until very recently, the Americans haven't been able to pull it off.

This style of play—a patient build up from deep in your own half, often featuring short passes forward as well as sideways or backward—is sometimes known as "playing out from the back," and it has become a hallmark of some of the greatest teams on the planet in the last 20 years. It requires a high level of skill, vision, patience, and composure. Teams that play in this style demand that everyone on the field, including defenders and even the goalkeeper, are highly proficient with the ball at their feet. Players need to have complete control over the ball in order to find their teammates with passes, dribble themselves out of trouble, and take accurate shots on goal. The great teams make it look easy but most teams make it look hard, because it is. Teams trying and failing to play the ball out of the back often give the ball away in front of their own goal, or find themselves desperately punting long balls into random areas of the field when the defensive pressure is too much. Like a dog biting at water from a garden hose, many teams grasp for this style hoping to capture it, but more often than not they come away with neither nourishment nor satisfaction.

Before anyone in the above passage of play was born, Howard Schultz went to 500 espresso bars in Milan. In 1985, Schultz was spinning up his own chain of specialty coffee shops in the Seattle area and he was convinced espresso was the future of coffee in America. Having just parted ways with a boutique coffee roaster called Starbucks (the owners weren't convinced espresso drinks would work in America), he was sampling Italian coffee in Milan because he was ready to bring a European coffee experience to the States. After raising money from small investors, Schultz opened Il Giornale, an espresso-serving coffee shop with limited seating and opera music playing in the background. Two successful years later, Schultz bought the Starbucks retail business, and after 30 even more successful years, most Starbucks locations in America were only about a mile away from another Starbucks location.

In the story of modern-day coffee in America there are generally considered to be three eras or "waves." The first wave began in the late 1800s, when coffee first became popular with European colonizers of the New World. Eventually coffee grew to be popular enough that brands like Folgers and Maxwell House became household names, with the latter reigning as the most popular brand in America for nearly a century. The second wave began in the 1960s, when Peet's Coffee & Tea began to treat the coffee business more like the wine business. They sourced unique beans from all over the world, blending and roasting them with a focus on flavor and quality. Second wave coffee roasters often preferred to import Arabica beans, which are grown in the tropics and produce uniquely flavorful coffee. Perfected by Starbucks in the 1990s, the second wave also made coffee a social phenomenon, opening big retail locations in which people could sit and talk with friends for hours over a Cinnamon Roll Frappuccino and listen to Paula Cole. The third wave followed shortly thereafter, and is known for an even greater attention to quality, taste, and detail. Not only are raw materials incredibly important, but the pulling of espresso shots and the steaming and stretching of milk are essential to the third-wave experience. If you don't mind spending $5.50 on your oat milk cappuccino, you're a fan of third wave coffee.

In the story of the United States Men's National Team, there are no waves. American soccer swells, it grows and moves but it never crests. Watching from a distance you might have seen what appeared to be the peak of wave: when Tim Howard blocked everything the Belgians could kick at him in the 2014 World Cup quarter finals, or when the Americans somehow advanced out of their group in the 1994 tournament being played at home for the first time, or when Landon Donovan tapped in a game-winner to advance in 2010. But as big as they were, those swells wouldn't become big enough to reach a tipping point, curl, and carry millions of giddy American sports fans with them to shore. They'd gradually lose momentum, crash quietly and sink back into the sea, waiting another four years to rise again.

Another four years later, the 2022 World Cup is on the horizon. The signs of another wave are appearing, and there are plenty of reasons to believe that the USMNT is better than ever. More Americans play at the highest level in Europe than ever before. Last year Christian Pulisic won the Champions League title with Chelsea FC and proved to be a valuable member of their team—not just a token American used to stoke interest overseas. Weston Mckennie is a regular starter for Italy's Juventus and often played alongside Cristiano Ronaldo (the idea that an American could share a field with Ronaldo week-in and week-out was unimaginable just a few years ago). There's even an American manager leading a Premier League team (two if you count Ted Lasso).

In every facet, there has never been a better time to be a soccer fan in America. With access to more games than ever on TV, from leagues all over the world, it's never been easier to spend entire weekends watching the Bundesliga or forming opinions on which Italian

Will midfielder Weston Mckennie brew something Americans will love in the 2022 World Cup?

Serie A rivalries are the most intense. The American professional leagues continue to grow and evolve as well, with men's and women's teams improving their play on the field and providing excellent experiences for fans in the stadium. Just as Howard Schultz predicted in the '90s as he stepped up to his 500th Milanese espresso bar, America seems to be ready for a new experience.

Global soccer's first wave coincided with the very beginnings of the game, as it was invented in

England and spread through the UK, making it the preferred sport of millions. A second wave began to crest after World War II, as more and more people around the world began to play and watch local club teams compete against each other. The 1950 World Cup was the first to include the world's best national teams, marking when soccer truly became the world's game. The third wave of soccer crested in the 1990s, as Italy's Serie A became the best league on the planet and heavily recruited players from all over Europe and South America. Just like the post-Folgers coffee business, these teams relied on the finest materials from around the world. This trend continues today, as the best teams spend extreme amounts of cash on the most highly regarded players, fueled by huge television rights contracts and seemingly never ending supplies of oil money.

If a wave is going to break in America this World Cup, it will rise from the same elements that have powered coffee's success over the years: ingredients and craftsmanship. America's raw materials are as good as ever, with players featuring for high-profile European clubs after spending years training in overseas youth academies. But this isn't entirely new—America has had a number of players find success in Europe over the last 30 years. What's different now is the craftsmanship. Non-goals like the passage described earlier (from a friendly match against Morocco), while still somewhat uncommon and awkward, give Americans hope that this group of talented, hard working young folks have sampled enough espresso in European coffee bars to begin the swells of a Starbucks-sized soccer wave that lands on American shores.

As the USMNT grinds its way through the CONCACAF qualification process to the 2022 World Cup, we see glimpses of a future filled with non-goals. One example is this delightful no-look split pass from Gio Reyna, a key player for Germany's Borussia Dortmund and one of America's most highly-regarded young players. For years Americans have been known as physical, industrious players—big, strong, hard working. When Americans have done well in European leagues, it's largely been on the fringes of the field, where they can use their speed and power to make themselves valuable. But Reyna represents a new kind of American player—highly skillful and creative with the ball at his feet, connecting defense to attack at the center of the game. Pulisic falls into this category too, as does Tyler Adams of Germany's RB Leipzig. The USMNT will rely on this core of creative talent in 2022, and, along with Mckennie, this group of young players (none are older than 24, Reyna is 19) is the most talented America has ever had. The ingredients are, finally, among the best in the world.

At times, the craftsmanship is also on par with the best. While the combination of raw materials and craft could potentially lead to wins, it certainly leads to non-goals that we haven't seen from American teams in the past. In a qualification game against Panama in early 2022, Reyna gave us a preview of what we might see more of in the World Cup. After a short clearance from Panama, Reyna receives the ball outside the top of the box. Moving laterally, he shields the ball from the light pressure of Panama's midfield, and then does his best Magic Johnson-to-James Worthy to find Luca de la Torre with a diabolical look-away pass through two Panamanian defenders. Reyna freezes the Panama back line with his eye contact on Pulisic out wide. He keeps his eyes on Pulisic but Reyna knows he wants to find the cutting de la Torre instead. Waiting until the defense has been stretched as much as possible, Reyna cuts a straight line of a pass through the opening he

Gio Reyna's no-look non-goal.

made with his look-away, straight to de la Torre's back foot. He turns and hits a short pass across the box to striker Jesus Ferreira, who can't get his feet settled in time and hits a shot over the crossbar. Goal or no goal, it's third wave soccer. It's the kind of play we might see Liverpool's Thiago make as his team carves up a lower-level Premier League opponent. It's the kind of play Reyna often makes for Dortmund. It's exactly what the USMNT needs to create their first wave.

MANCHESTER CITY:
OR, THE WHALE

Whether or not you've read Herman Melville's *Moby Dick*, you probably know the story. A deranged, peg-legged sea captain, seeking revenge on the whale that took his limb, drives his ship and crew to ruin while ultimately failing to kill his target. That's the story. But *Moby Dick* is about so much more than that. Published just before the American Civil War and written during the fractious years leading up to it, *Moby Dick* is an adventure at sea, a meditation on the wonders of the natural world, an examination of man's moral liquidity, and lots more. Between the plot points, which are honestly pretty few and far between, Melville delights the reader with detailed descriptions of whaling vessel construction, chapters-long digres-

Manchester City manager Pep Guardiola at sea.

sions on the physiology and grandeur of whales, along with pre-Darwin conjecture on the prehistoric origins of the animal world and man's relationship with it. And this is why Melville's masterpiece makes an appearance in a book that is ostensibly about soccer: *Moby Dick* is legendary not for the plot but for everything but the plot. We read *Moby Dick* for the journey. We read it to see the world through the eyes of its narrator Ishmael—a young man in search of adventure, open to new experiences, searching for the non-goals of life.

As Ishmael puts it, "I am tormented with an everlasting itch for things remote. I love to sail forbidden sea, and land on barbarous coasts." And it's this openness that leads Ishmael to Queequeg: a tattoo covered, idol-worshiping harpooner from a fictional South Pacific island, although that title doesn't quite do him justice. Calling Queequeg a harpooner is like calling Cristiano Ronaldo a soccer player. Queequeg was a once-in-a-lifetime harpooning legend adept at hitting his target from unreasonable distances and was equally as good at carving and dismembering his prey, just as Ronaldo might filet the carcasses of his opponents with a salacious goal celebration. Despite their surface-level differences Queequeg and Ishmael quickly became friends—their bond sustaining them through the journey aboard Ahab's ship the Pequod, sailing in search of whales, in search of adventure, and in service of a captain so driven by his own vision of success that he sacrifices everything to achieve it.

We can see echoes of this journey in the voyages of the soccer team known as Manchester City. A prolifically successful team in recent years, City sets sail every August to create goals and capture victory, returning in May with the spoils of their success in staggering amounts of wins and treasure. Commanded by a captain well known for his single-minded focus, not just on victory but on perfection, City embark on their missions not only to win but to win beautifully, and they often do. But City's manager, the Spaniard Pep Guardiola, is haunted by his own white whale—the UEFA Champions League title. While Guardiola has won the Champions League trophy twice as manager of FC Barcelona, he's never won it with City, and with each final, semi-final, or group-stage elimination the shadow of the trophy appears to grow larger in his mind. City consistently win the English Premier League season title, but success in Europe has been as elusive as Ahab's Moby Dick. Voyage after voyage, Guardiola can't seem to capture the trophy he most desperately seeks.

City attack with patience, skill, and precision. Guardiola's obsession with perfection gives City a unique playing style that lends the air of a global circumnavigation to every possession. Each of their players, from their corvette-like strikers to their gunship defenders, is comfortable with the ball at their feet, enabling the team to string together passes and dribbles that pull and stretch defenses apart for minutes at a time, exhausting their opponents like a fisherman might exhaust a hooked fish that isn't ready to be dinner. These uncommon attacking voyages yield a near-constant stream of non-goals. Long stretches of possession reveal the genius and expertise of the City players, featuring prodigious creativity on the ball and delicious passes from midfield to attack. When they do occasionally lose the ball, their collective tenacity ensures that they win it back before their opponents can come up for air. It's because of this style that Guardiola's City teams have proven to be one of the most reliable non-goal creating forces in modern soccer, and like Melville's *Moby Dick*, City are Guardiola's masterpiece.

At this point soccer fans know the plot of a Manchester City game: they win in the end, and no team has captured more points in a Premier League season than City (in 2017-18 they earned a record-setting 100 points). If Guardiola is Ahab in this soccer story, then we, the viewers, are Ishmael. If we come to our televisions every weekend morning as Ishmael would— open to new experiences, itching for adventure—we'll discover the beauty and the majesty of soccer as Ishmael discovered the transcendent glory of the whale.

We'll encounter fascinating players from all corners of the globe and feats of skill the most lethal harpooner would appreciate. And it's possible that, like readers of *Moby Dick*, we'll come to understand that the voyage itself is really the best part. Appreciating the journey opens our eyes to the non-goals we'll see when we look beyond outcomes like goals and wins. Watching soccer for non-goals ensures that we'll come home with enough treasure for a lifetime, and we'll avoid the outcome-focused torture Ahab endures tour after tour.

Like all voyages at sea, City's have a beginning, middle and an end. But unlike the on-field voyages of many other teams, City's often take a circuitous path to their destination. That's not to say they don't arrive at their desired port (City once again scored more goals than any other Premier League team in the 2021-2022 season), but they might chart a different course than most, moving back as often as forward, retracing their steps, returning to where they began, making new plans as they go, and following the wind as they create an ocean's worth of non-goals. Guardiola's plans often begin with his own luxuriously tattooed marksman, the Brazilian goalkeeper Ederson. Known as much for instigating attacks with his feet as stopping them with

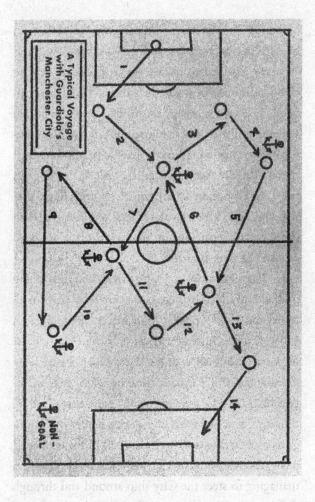

A Typical Voyage with Guardiola's Manchester City

NON-GOAL

managing to steer the City ship around and abruptly

let everyone be plays a perfectly weighted pass to a

his hands, there isn't a goalkeeper in the world that can match Ederson's passing ability. With the power and accuracy required to place a 60-yard pass at the foot of his teammate in stride (he's the first goalkeeper in City's history to register an assist), but with enough skill and guile to dribble himself out of trouble, Ederson begins attacks in the way Melville's harpooner ends them—lethally and without mercy. NGPG (non-goals per game) is not an actual statistic, but it's likely that with his feet Ederson creates at least one non-goal each game, certainly placing him amongst the best non-goal creating keepers in history.

The next stop in a City voyage is often in the midfield. Manned by players that are both jacks of all trades and masters of all, a Manchester City midfield is no place for an unseasoned sailor. Two of City's most important midfielders of the last several years are Ilkay Gundiguan and Kevin DeBruyne, who each maintain high NGPG averages while taking turns leading the team in actual goals and assists. DeBruyne's non-goals usually take place in the middle of the field as he navigates treacherous water with skill and experience, managing to steer the City ship around and through defenses until he plays a perfectly weighted pass to a teammate or finishes the attack on his own. His excellence with either foot makes him Guardiola's de facto first mate, the perfect executor of the captain's vision and a non-goal machine the likes of which are not often seen. Gundoguan, on the other hand, slides alongside DeBruyne like a remora follows a shark, always nearby and ready to create in the shadows. Gundoguan has certainly scored some big goals for City, including two championship-clinching goals on the final day of the 2022 season, but his movement on and off the ball, his ability to cover back on defense to regain possession, and his instinctual movement into open space give him opportunities to create non-goals from shore to shore.

While City's course may see them return to their own third of the field or even back into the original port of departure, eventually, inevitably, the ball ends up at the destination: the back of their opponent's net. On a whaling ship, hitting the target would be the job of the harpooner: a big, physically strong character able to hurl a massive spear many yards over the ocean, impaling an enormous marine mammal and tracking it to its death. But Manchester City are a deadly team that lacks a traditional killer. They prefer to hunt in packs, as smaller creatures work together to create a feeding frenzy that brings down whales like a pride of lions taking down an elephant. This has been a hallmark of Guardiola's career as a manager, winning an incredible number of titles, often without the typical harpooning striker. Luckily for the enlightened viewer, this means City have to create non-goals in order to score their actual goals. Take, for example, the sprightly attacker Bernardo Silva. Slight of build and fleet of foot, Bernardo's dexterity and flair for showmanship produce lovely first touches that outfox overeager defenders and sublime escape acts that run opponents in circles. Without a big striker to overpower opponents, City teams have become the best at bewildering opposition with non-goals in quick succession as they patiently and skillfully make their way across the ocean on their way to victory. This is essentially what makes Manchester City the non-goal whale that they are in 2022. Driven by a manager obsessed with goals, they've built a system that relies on non-goals to create them. Outwardly concerned only with outcomes— the biggest plot points of any soccer game—Manchester City have composed a style of play that makes the moments between goals as rich as any adventure novel.

*Bernardo Silva playing catch and release
with a defender.*

There's more to learn from *Moby Dick* as Melville explores the nature of humans and their relationship with each other and the natural world: the characteristics and variety of whales, the means by which humans go about killing and harvesting the largest and most majestic animal on the planet (one that evolved from a dog-like creature 50 million years ago, at first tip-toeing into a body of water, then learning to swim and hunt comfortably there, eventually spending more and more time underwater as the position of its nose moved higher and further back on its body until it became a spout on its back, slowly growing larger and larger generation after generation until it came to weigh over 90,000 pounds), the relationship between people, wealth, and what they claim to own, and our willingness to mine the earth for our own profit. These themes are also relevant to any conversation concerning Manchester City. Funded by the oil-rich billionaire and member of the ruling family of Abu Dhabi, Mansour bin Zayed Al Nahyan, City have virtually unlimited funds at their disposal to buy the best players in the world, state-of-the-art equipment for their team, and glittering stadiums and practice facilities. The fact that their fortune comes directly from the earth itself might have amused Melville, yet it might have fallen to Ishmael to sum up humanity's own obsession with success as he did aboard the Pequod: "For there is no folly of the beast of the earth which is not infinitely outdone by the madness of men." As you become more familiar with non-goals it's good to know where they come from, and to understand how they're made. Without looking under the surface of the game there's no way to truly appreciate it—the good, the bad, and the mad.

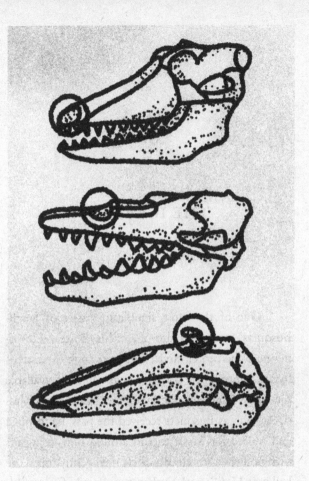

Evolution of a whale's nose placement. Top: Pakicetus;
Middle: Rodhocetus nostrils moved higher on the skull;
Bottom: A modern gray whale with spout on back.

THE ICEBERG

One of the most significant passes of Sergio Busquets' career was also one of his shortest. Hovering near the center circle, Busquets took three steps forward into open space to make himself available for a pass from his teammate, the great Lionel Messi. As soon as Busquets received the pass, he stopped and waited for Messi to run around him, using his own body as a screen. Busquets then gently rolled the ball into Messi's path so that it was just in front of his favored left foot—the ball only traveling about the length of its own diameter. Messi gathered steam and neither his defender, who had been screened out by Busquets' positioning, nor Busquets' defender, who was late covering, could slow him down. Four more defenders and a goalkeeper stood between Messi and the goal, and Messi beat them all. Neatly dribbling past the first two defenders in his way and flying past the third, he rounded his way toward the goal and rolled the ball past the sprawling keeper as the fourth defender tried to get a foot on the ball and missed. Together, Messi and Busquets turned what was essentially a 2-on-7 into a game-clinching goal for Barcelona against their biggest rivals, Real Madrid.

In explaining his "Iceberg Theory" of writing, Ernest Hemingway once said, "If a writer of prose knows enough about what he is writing about he may omit things that he knows and the reader, if the writer is writing truly enough, will have a feeling of those things as strongly as though the writer had stated them." Rather than flaunt his vocabulary and mastery of the English language with complex, decorative language, Hemingway believed that a story could actually be stronger if an author intentionally omitted elements that could easily have been included. These omissions ensure only the most "true" information appears on the page, allowing the reader to feel or imagine the subtexts lying below the story's surface. With this approach, and through his signature use of

Sergio Busquets's expertise lies deep below the surface of the game.

simple and plain language, Hemingway became one of the most distinctive writers of the 20th century.

To Hemingway, it was crucial that the writer understood his or her subject matter completely. This understanding allows the writer the freedom of telling the story efficiently, letting the reader absorb the truth and paint their own picture through the few carefully chosen words on the page. The power of an iceberg lies not in just what appears on the surface.

Soccer is full of players that perform at surface

level. These players create moments that are impossible to miss: goals, penalties, feats of superhuman athleticism, post-goal shirt removal, et cetera. The Mbappes, Salahs, Haalands, Son Heung-mins of the world command attention. Their speed and movement, their ability on the ball, the frequency at which they demand slow-motion replays and closeups from camera crews make their presence on the field utterly conspicuous. Their strengths and interests are visible to any viewer, and they fill their time on the ball with every trick in the book: stepovers, fakes, dribbles, hesitation, acceleration, Cruyff turns, Ronaldo chops. Their brilliance lies in the visible realm. The list of these players is long and reads like a greatest hits collection of the last 20 years, from "Aguerooooooo!" to Zidane.

But there's a much shorter list of players whose genius lies below the surface of the water, deep underneath the frozen, fractured peak, reaching so far down it's almost impossible to see without pressurized cabins and depth-rated lights. These are players with impeccable technical skills that they appear to not actually use on a regular basis. Players with body shapes one might not associate with elite athletes. Players that have made careers of behind the scenes non-goal craftsmanship, churning out spectacular moments that you might miss if you don't have your spyglass at the ready, looking beyond the surface for something lying deeper.

At the top of this depth-dwelling list is Sergio Busquets. Born in Barcelona and belonging professionally only to FC Barcelona during his long career, he is a study in consistency. A master of efficient movement, an unrivaled anticipator, and unquestionably the slowest guy on the field at any given time, Busquets' limited physical gifts require heightened mental and instinctual performance. Like a bat maneuvering through echolocation, Busquets has become one of the best midfielders of his generation as an archetypal under-the-surface player—anticipating and intercepting opposition passes with tactics that aren't always visible to the naked eye.

Almost everything Busquets does is unremarkable at first glance. For example, most players use their skills on the ball to get past an opponent and move toward the goal; Busquets is more likely to use his limited but effective repertoire to escape pressure and find space moving backward or sideways. While many players want the ball so they can carry it forward un-

Would Hemingway have displayed the "grace under pressure" he so admired had he joined the Barcelona midfield?

til they're forced to give it up, Busquets wants the ball only so he can deliver it safely to someone in a better position. His instinct and experience lead him to use the sparest of language when others would indulge in paragraphs of ornate description or flowery dribbling. Messi's goal mentioned above was brilliant, but it was anything but an individual effort. It was made possible by the iceberg on the field. So many other players would have engaged in a thesaurus of movement, attempting to fill the page with their own soccer logor-rhea. Busquets knows his subject matter so well, he's free to present his ideas in the most delicate, elegantly crafted stories in contemporary soccer—revealing only the truth and allowing the viewer to absorb and enjoy the result.

Playing as a "pivot" player in Barcelona's three-man midfield, Busquets is responsible for defending his defenders. Playing centrally, Busquets stops attacks before they have a chance to begin, but not by obvious physicality, strength, or speed (his only physical gift is a pair of abnormally long legs, which he uses primarily for interception). Rather, Busquets relies on years of experience playing at the highest level to position him-self in the right area of the field before disaster strikes. This honed sense of anticipation gives Busquets an edge most players don't have. And in his role, this edge is much more valuable than a high top speed or pow-erful physicality.

This style of play won't often make a highlight reel, but it is essential to the style preferred by Barce-lona and the Spanish national team. A style which, over the last 15 years, has raked in an unprecedented amount of success. The Spain team was the first to

Busquets makes two tackles in quick succession.
Years of experience not pictured.

win three successive major championships: the 2008 Euro, the 2010 World Cup, and the 2012 Euro, with Busquets playing major roles in 2010 and 2012 (including every minute of those tournaments). For Barcelona, he's won every imaginable trophy multiple times, including three Champions League and eight Spanish La Liga titles.

In the example above, Busquets anticipates his way to two tackles in quick succession, using his unusually long legs to win the ball not once but twice. This deep understanding of the game allows Busquets to omit surface-level defensive histrionics. He doesn't need to sprint and catch up to an opponent to win the ball from behind, he'd rather put out fires at the first sign of a spark. This kind of defensive play also becomes the beginning of his team's attack. By winning the ball back quickly and high up the field, Busquets can keep Barcelona in a good position, ready to strike. This kind of defense-to-offense play is a fundamental non-goal. Blink and you might miss it, but the impact is often seen in the actual goals that come as a direct result. Rarely has a slower player beaten so many faster players while on the ball. Busquets is a man without a "turbo" button, so he uses other players' speed and ambition against them. It often happens like this:

- A Barcelona player passes the ball to Busquets.

- An opposing player sprints to pressure Busquets before he has time to control the ball.

- Before he receives the pass, Busquets positions his body so that it appears that he'll move to his right.

- The defender approaches quickly, enthusiastically believing he'll steal the ball from the slow-moving Busquets.

- With one simple and elegant touch of the ball, Busquets plays the ball to his left—a minimalist maneuver into space that evades the defender and gives him time to begin an attack, leaving the overly-aggressive defender in his wake.

It's not flashy. It's not obviously impressive, but

A typical Busquets slow-motion change of direction.

it's Busquets. Many of the things one expects of a soccer player in 2022—running around at high speed,
flashy footwork, jumping high into the air, a stylish
haircut, scoring goals, elaborate celebrations—have
all been omitted. Only the most "true" elements of
the game remain, strengthening his team by leaving
out the inessential. As his former manager Vicente del
Bosque has said, "If you watch the whole game, you
won't see Busquets—but watch Busquets, and you
will see the whole game." Like an iceberg, Busquets'
power comes from unknowable depths.

2022 NON-GOAL
WORLD CUP PREVIEW

As the World Cup 2022 approaches, humanity will once again be treated to a month-long festival of non-goals. And not just from the Brazilians, Germans or Italians (wait, nevermind) of the world, but from the tiny Costa Ricans, the bulldogging Uruguayans, and maybe even the scrappy, young, incredibly hard-working but not-always-that-skillful Americans. While it's very difficult to predict outcomes in the World Cup, it's more reasonable to predict non-goal generation based on past performance of national teams and their players throughout the club season.

In no particular order, and after an typically informal and unscientific review of recent performance, these are the teams likely to lead the non-goal creation in this year's tournament.

- Belgium: Commentators have been talking about Belgium's "golden generation" for a while now, but even if they might have missed their window for a championship, any team with Kevin De Bruyne running the show will deliver a steady supply of non-goal action. Look for KDB to combine with fellow midfielder Youri Tielemans and crafty forward Dries Mertens in areas near their opponents' goal.

- Spain: Rolling out their most exciting line-up in several years, Spain will continue their evolution away from the "tiki-taka" style of the 2010s and into the direct, fast-paced attacking play that took them to the semi-finals of 2021's 2020 Euro Cup. FC Barcelona's Pedri has emerged as a world-class creative force in midfield, generating forward-thinking attacking moves that save Barcelona from their sometimes sleepy horizontal passing play. Joined by fellow

Kevin De Bruyne is undoubtedly the finest Belgian of his generation.

Barcelona teammates Gavi, Ansu Fati, and Ferran Torres in attack, this is a young squad with lots of non-goal potential. Iceberg Sergio Busquets anchors the team with his placid yet inventive brand of under-the-surface genius in what might be his last international tournament appearance.

- England: Not usually at the top of the list for non-goal creation, England has recently undergone a transformation. From booted long-balls to possession-based play, English teams of the last few years have been much more fun to watch than in years past. Largely responsible for this change in style is a dynamic cast of young players trained in combination play. Forward and goal scorer Harry Kane is also arguably the team's best passer. Midfielder Mason Mount has proven to be a legitimate source of non-goals at Chelsea. If James Ward-Prowse makes the final squad he'll be one of the best set-piece technicians in the tournament. Highly-skilled youngster Phil Foden will delight non-goal fans with his clever dribbling and passes into space.

• Argentina: La Albiceleste ("The White and Sky Blue") has been a frustrating team to watch since Leo Messi ascended to the throne of world's greatest player in the 2010s. While the world flocked to their television sets to behold Messi's brilliance, it seemed as if his teammates were just as happy to watch him play—often looking more like observers than active participants in the tournament. Messi was incredible enough to somehow make it work on his own, dragging the lifeless body of the Argentinean team to the final in 2014 and the round of 16 in 2018. But what's exciting about Argentina in 2022 is that as Messi slows down, his supporting cast is stepping up. Joined by midfielder Giovani Lo Celso (a key player in Villareal's surprising trip to the Champions League semi-finals) and lively winger Lucas Ocampos, Messi hasn't been the only creative force on the field. Add to the mix speedy striker Lautaro Martinez and Argentina will likely be one of the most prolific non-goal-creating teams in Qatar.

- Denmark: After their incredible Euro Cup performance in 2021, in which they saw their best player suffer a cardiac arrest on the field and recover, then played their way into the semi-finals, Denmark is no longer a dark horse. With Christian Eriksen playing beautifully in England after his on-field heart attack, Pierre-Emile Hojbjerg and Thomas Delaney supporting him in midfield, and strikers Mikkel Damsgaard and Joakim Maehle rounding out the attack, this team won't surprise anyone with their non-goal output.

ACKNOWLEDGEMENTS

I started talking about non-goals with Kyler Brown in the summer of 2021, just after the Euro cup tournament. Thank you, sir, for always being an enthusiastic idea partner—maybe we should get a podcast going.

Thank you to my wife Katie, for supporting me and my ridiculous ideas, and for talking me out of comparing Luka Modric to Wolfgang Puck.

I'd like to especially thank my subject matter experts. Tom Gilmartin lent his expertise in American history to the "noble train of artillery" chapter, Ian Goode helped me avoid writing a book report on

Moby Dick, and Greg Ahlbach educated me on the true characteristics of third wave coffee. Nick Greene generously answered unsolicited emails with guidance on how to describe on-field action while making sure you're having a good time doing it.

I owe a double album of thanks to my editor Ryan Pinkard, for taming the wild em dash and for his graceful, Guardiola-like steering into fruitful non-goal territory.

Thanks to the good folks at American Soccer Analysis, including Drew Olsen, Carlon Carpenter, and Jamon Moore, for sharing their illuminating data on goals.

RECOMMENDED READING

Janna Levin, *Black Hole Survival Guide*
Stephen Greenblatt, *The Swerve*
Umberto Eco, *How to Write a Thesis*
Bill Buford, *Heat*
Stephen Shore, *Modern Instances*
Herman Melville, *Moby Dick*
Giuseppe Tomasi di Lampedusa, *The Leopard*
Ovid, *Metamorphoses*
Edith Hamilton, *Mythology*
Nick Greene, *How to Watch Basketball Like A Genius*
Ross King, *Brunelleschi's Dome*

ABOUT THE AUTHOR

Bob Bjarke is an FC Barcelona fan living in Oakland, California. When he's not watching every minute of Barcelona's season on television, Bob is an advertising and marketing creative professional, a pasta enthusiast, a husband and father, an assistant youth soccer coach, and an avid hobbyist.

NOTES

NOTES